Copyright © 1999 by Albin Michel Jeunesse.
English translation copyright © 1999 by Chronicle Books.
First published in French by Albin Michel Jeunesse under the title "Didou Sait Tout".
Published by arrangement with Albin Michel Jeunesse.

English edition type design by Paul Donald.
Typeset in Jennerik and ITC Bailey Sans.
Printed in France.

Library of Congress Cataloging-in-Publication Data
Got, Yves.
[Didou sait tout. English]
Sam's first word book / by Yves Got.
p. cm.
"First published in French by Albin Michel Jeunesse under the title 'Didou Sait
Tout'"—T.p. verso.
Includes index.
ISBN 0-8118-2615-5
1. Vocabulary—Juvenile literature.   [1. Vocabulary.]
I. Title.
PE1449 .G6413 2000
428.1--dc21
00-031505

Distributed in Canada by Raincoast Books
9050 Shaughnessy Street, Vancouver, British Columbia V6P 6E5

10 9 8 7 6 5 4 3

Chronicle Books LLC
85 Second Street, San Francisco, California 94105

www.chroniclebooks.com/Kids

Sam's First Word Book

by Yves Got

chronicle books · san francisco

baby

pacifier

rattle

Mom

Dad

brothers
and sisters

grandparents

crib

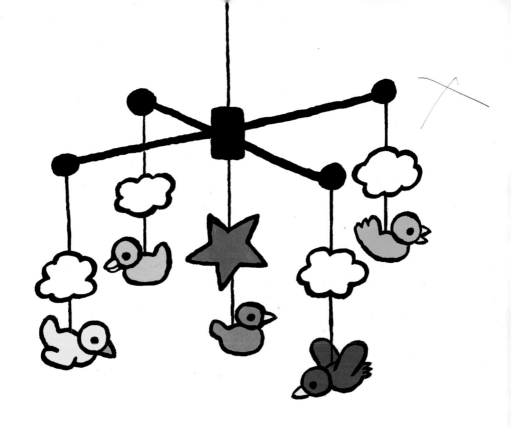

mobile

music box

drum

pull toy

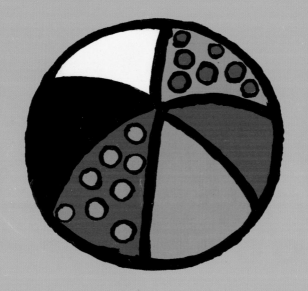

ball

teddy bear

blankie

tricycle

doll

convertible

train

clown

puppet

blocks

push-cart

book

paint

computer

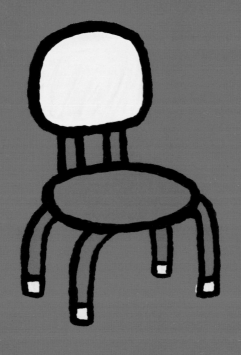

chair

toy chest

helicopter

garbage can

vacuum cleaner

refrigerator

washing machine

high chair

table

pot

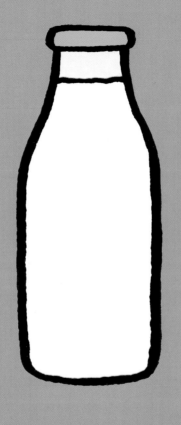

bottle

bib

baby bottle

fork and spoon

jar

cracker

cup

carrot

bowl

egg

tomato

banana

strawberry

potty

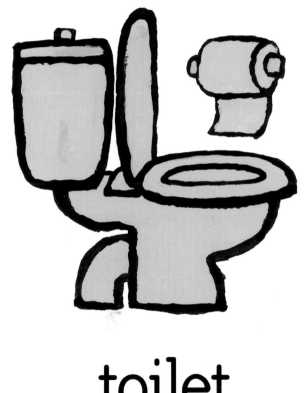

toilet

sink

toothbrush

hairbrush

mirror

bathtub

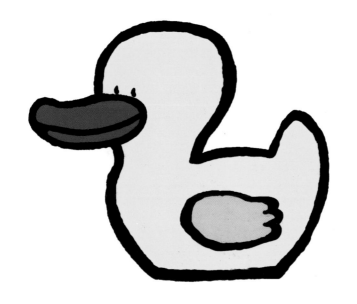

rubber ducky

diaper

onesie

T-shirt

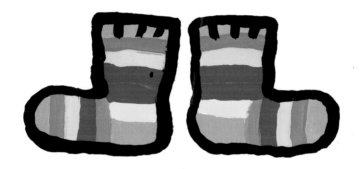

socks

pajamas

slippers

overalls

dress

snowsuit

mittens

shoes

cap

boots

raincoat

house

window

clouds

umbrella

key

door

fire truck

motorcycle

bus

crane

shopping cart

backpack

stroller

pail, shovel
and rake

bouncy ride

slide

flowers

butterfly

tree

bird

balloons

bench

doctor

medicine

clay

puzzle

coatrack

goldfish

bed

alarm clock

telephone

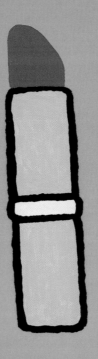

lipstick

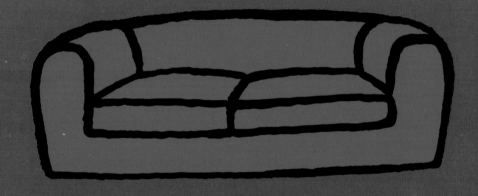

couch

TV and
remote control

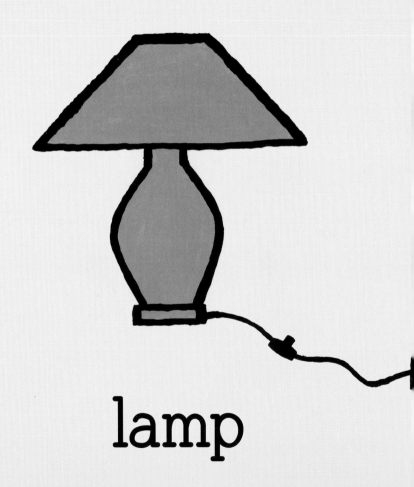

lamp

armchair

birthday cake

camera

presents

Christmas tree

car

car seat

airplane

suitcase

beach umbrella

sun

bathing suit
and sunglasses

water wings

cat

mouse

spider

ladybug

turtle

sheep

COW

chicken

zebra

crocodile

lion

elephant

summary

Sam's Family
(pages 7 to 13)

baby
pacifier
rattle
Mom
Dad
brothers and sisters
grandparents

Sam's Room
(pages 14 to 35)

crib
mobile
music box
drum
pull toy
ball
teddy bear
blankie
tricycle
doll
convertible
train
clown
puppet

blocks
push-cart
book
paint
computer
chair
toy chest
helicopter

The Kitchen
(pages 36 to 43)

garbage can
vaccuum cleaner
refrigerator
washing machine
high chair
table
pot
bottle

Eating
(pages 44 to 55)

bib
baby bottle
fork and spoon
jar

cracker
cup
carrot
bowl
egg
tomato
banana
strawberry

In the Bathroom
(pages 56 to 63)

potty
toilet
sink
toothbrush
hairbrush
mirror
bathtub
rubber ducky

Getting Dressed
(pages 64 to 77)

diaper
onesie
T-shirt
socks
pajamas
slippers
overalls
dress
snowsuit
mittens
shoes
cap
boots
raincoat

Going Outside
(pages 78 to 89)

house
window
clouds
umbrella
key
door
fire truck

index